I'M BEING TARGETED BY A GANG.

NOW WHAT?

MARTIN GITLIN

ROSEN PUBLISHING®

New York

Published in 2017 by The Rosen Publishing Group, Inc.
29 East 21st Street, New York, NY 10010

Copyright © 2017 by The Rosen Publishing Group, Inc.

First Edition

Library of Congress Cataloging-in-Publication Data

Names: Gitlin, Marty, author.
Title: I'm being targeted by a gang : now what? / Martin Gitlin.
Description: New York : Rosen Publishing, 2017. | Series: Teen life 411 | Includes bibliographical references and index.
Identifiers: LCCN 2016027962 | ISBN 9781508171911 (library bound)
Subjects: LCSH: Gangs—Juvenile literature. | Self-perception—Juvenile literature.
Classification: LCC HV6437 .G58 2017 | DDC 364.106/6—dc23
LC record available at https://lccn.loc.gov/2016027962

Manufactured in Malaysia

CONTENTS

They are hanging out behind the school. Or in the alley across the street. Or in the parking lot of your favorite fast-food joint.

They are gang members. And they want to recruit you. They hope you are captivated by their lifestyle. They target kids they believe to be dissatisfied with their lives. They talk to those who have been bullied at school or who have had discipline problems. Or the ones with unsatisfying home lives.

They're eager to impress you. They're trying to make you feel that they can be your family. They offer you protection from those you fear. They promise you can make more money as a gang member than working a job most common with teenagers. They draw you in with bits of gang knowledge or history that they believe will intrigue you.

Perhaps they have invited you to a party where they have shown you jewelry and cash. There might be drugs, alcohol, or weapons there. Gang members think that is cool and hope you think so too. What they will not tell you is that they had to rob and steal to get what they wanted. They had to commit acts of violence. Maybe some of their friends have ended up dead.

You might be confused. You might be scared. But the more you learn about gangs and gang life, the more you will realize the physical and emotional risk they bring.

Beware of gang members who seek to recruit others by making their lifestyle sound fun and exciting—it's more dangerous than anything else.

Life on the streets is often "kill or be killed" for gang members.

Gangs can never be your family. Family members care about each other. Gang members only care about what you can do for them. If they cared about you, they wouldn't allow you to commit crimes that put your very life in danger.

There are resources available to you. Your friends, family members, school counselors, teachers, coaches, clergy, and police officers are positive influences in your life who can prove invaluable when you are being targeted by a gang. Know that they *want* to help. So do task forces and other community groups that work to nudge young people in the right direction and out of gangs.

The most important person who can help you is you. Take pride in yourself and your future. Think and act for yourself. Choose your friends wisely. If they are asking you to commit crimes or put yourself at risk, they're not your friends.

Show your potential by performing well in school. The seeds for a bright, happy, and prideful future can be planted in the classroom. Pursue a fulfilling hobby such as a sport or afterschool activity that you enjoy. And getting a real job to make money can instill self-esteem and a strong work ethic that can last a lifetime. It can even launch your career.

There's much to know and much to learn. What needs to be clear from the start though is that joining a gang places you on a path to nowhere but misery, jail, and quite possibly the grave.

CHAPTER 1

NOTHING GOOD ABOUT GANGS

Life often ends quickly and violently for gang members. Every year, about two thousand gang members across the United States end up murdered. They fight over turf. They fight over drug money. They fight over what they perceive as pride.

Perhaps you have attended the funeral of a friend or relative who was gunned down in a gang-related shooting.

Hopefully, that experience convinced you to never join a gang. But for every victory in the war against youth violence, there has been a defeat. The battle against gangs has been raging for decades. The National Gang Center estimates that the total number of gang killings rose significantly from 2008 to 2012, and the 850,000 gang members in the country in 2012 represents the highest total since 1996.

The National Gang Center also indicates that gangs are most prevalent in cities with populations over one hundred thousand. The problem is also acute in rural counties, suburban areas, and smaller cities. There's no free zone for millions of young Americans who are candidates for gang membership. Their futures depend greatly on the decisions they make.

A survey cited by the National Institute of Justice taken in 2010 revealed that 45 percent of high school students and 35 percent of middle-schoolers report a gang presence in their schools. Nearly one in twelve surveyed admitted that they had belonged to a gang at some point.

The number of gang members has risen markedly heading into the second decade of the twenty-first century. Research has revealed that gangs are active in every city in the United States with more than 250,000 people and 85 percent of cities with populations of at least 100,000. The National Crime Council notes that gangs are responsible for nearly half of all violent crime in most areas, up to 90 percent

Watching friends get murdered and attending their funerals is often a sad reality for those who choose to participate in gang activity.

in such states as Arizona, California, Colorado, Illinois, and Texas.

Gang warfare has resulted in startling and disturbing numbers. The National Institute of Justice stated in 2010 that homicide is the second-leading cause of American adolescent deaths with an average of thirteen per day. But that doesn't tell the whole story. More than seven hundred thousand young people between the ages of fifteen and twenty-four were treated in emergency hospitals every year during the survey period because of gang violence.

Though murder has proved to be the tragic outcome of gang membership for thousands every year, other consequences can also lead to death. Gang members are at far greater risk than other kids to become addicted to drugs and alcohol. They're much more likely to become involved in sexual behavior that can result in disease and teen pregnancy. Statistics from the Office of Juvenile Justice and Delinquency Prevention show that they're also at a significantly higher risk of dropping out of school, experiencing family problems, and consistently losing jobs.

TRADING GOOD FOR BAD

A new gang member will cut ties with family, friends, schools and the religious community to focus on gang participation and identity. This process is called "knifing off." James C. Howell concluded in his overview of gang prevention that the onset of gang membership was associated with an 82 percent increase in criminal activity. The longer an individual remains in a gang, the more severe the effect becomes and the further distant he or she grows from healthy social relationships.

The more you learn about gangs, the more you will understand their potential danger. You should know about the juvenile behavior and risk factors for those who become the most likely candidates. You should know that kids are rarely pushed into gangs. Instead, they're lured by the promise of protection, money, family, and material gain before making a conscious choice to join. Some who join gangs simply believe it will be a more fun and exciting lifestyle. Another attraction is a friend or family member in the same gang.

The process generally begins with negative peer groups and social networks that form during earlier years of adolescence. That is the time when some youths become involved in "starter gangs" rather than hardcore violent gangs. This introduction to gang culture can include the use of gang rituals and symbols. Established gangs sometimes create their own starter groups of younger delinquents called "wannabes" or "juniors."

Teens should understand as well that the makeup of most gangs changes quickly and drastically. Unlike a healthy family— brothers and sisters for life with caring parents—gangs provide no stability. Not only are some gang members killed, but youths tend to drift in and out at a rapid pace. One survey of middle school students revealed that 35 percent of identified gangs had been

What is known as "gangsta rap" glorifies a negative lifestyle and can be a lure that increases gang membership.

around for one year or less and only 10 percent were said to have existed for eleven years or more.

The decision whether or not to join a gang is ultimately yours. But the more positive information you allow yourself to see and hear, the more likely you will make the right decision. And that does not only include advice from those you know.

It is definitely advisable to embrace guidance from family members and friends, as well as school counsellors, coaches and teachers. One should also listen to members of the community, such as law enforcement officials, about the dangers of joining a gang.

However, there are other outside influences that have

THE ULTIMATE ANTI-GANG RAP

Many rap and hip-hop artists have written and performed songs with an anti-gang message. Perhaps the most notable was a track in 1990 by the West Coast All-Stars, a collaboration of hip-hop artists, entitled "We're All in the Same Gang." The song targeted youth in Los Angeles, particularly those in the rival Crips and Bloods, the most notorious gangs in the United States.

The song was written to sway young people from joining gangs and reduce gang violence. The following, which speaks of the innocent victims of gang violence, are perhaps the most powerful lyrics:

One of our victims was a three-year-old girl

Well, you gang members, you still don't get it, do ya?

The song cites the "madness" of a straight A student throwing his life away by dropping out of school and robbing people to get money for drugs for himself and to sell. It also encourages gang bangers to get "presentable" and take a healthier path in life.

Such rap and hip-hop songs have played a role in combatting other music that glorifies gang life. Young people are encouraged by music that promotes a positive lifestyle, as opposed to songs that seek to inspire kids to join gangs, which may make them feel as though they have no other choices in life.

played a significant role in the decision-making process for youths weighing their options, including those coming from the media. You should be aware that the growth of gangs over the last two decades can be attributed to some extent to its adoration in popular culture. A prime influence is rap music, some of which glorify gang life while other of it seeks to convince youths to stay away. Teenagers facing the dilemma involving gang membership can tune in or tune out to such songs. Loved ones can only hope they make the right choice and listen only to songs that provide an anti-gang message.

The subgenre of rap music, commonly called gangsta rap, has glorified the gang lifestyle as glamorous and rewarding. Such negative propaganda should be rejected. Instead, listeners should embrace the many positive messages expressed by other musicians and celebrities.

Former gang member Derek Brown knows all about various negative influences. He was raised on the streets of Chicago, which has suffered more gang-related homicides than any other city in the United States in recent years. He runs a community organization called Boxing Out Negativity, an after-school boxing program for youth. He not only teaches kids in Chicago how to box, but he warns them against the dangers of listening to certain rap music lyrics and speaks on the subject in schools. He even checks homework to make sure students are on the right track in their education.

Brown is one of many ideal role models for troubled youth because he has lived the life of a gangbanger and understands better than anyone the negative and potentially fatal role it has on the lives of youths. Known as "Shotgun" as a gang member between the ages of 14 and 25, he was shot, stabbed, and imprisoned during that time. And he admits that gangstar rap absolutely influenced him.

He also knows that rap and hip hop music can send a positive message instead. He listened to such life-affirming artists such as Queen Latifah as a kid. But he eventually tuned them out and began listening to groups like N.W.A., which voiced violent anti-police and anti-women messages that helped lure him into gangs.

"I sold drugs, and I was making a living off it but not knowing the hurt I caused," explained Brown more than a decade after escaping gang life. "When they say it's blood money, they're right. I've had money with blood on it. I've had stinky money that had been in people's socks and in their (underwear). Some of had been stolen from their mother's purse, and the damage I did in my community was tremendous."

After Brown shot someone, he would listen to songs that made him feel proud of the havoc he had wrought. It was not until the age of nineteen, when his best friend was killed, that he began waking up to reality. Even though he was making money selling drugs, he was living in a roach-infested home with drug-addict neighbors. And though he finally gained a desire to leave the gang, he did not know how to do it safely. He simply advises others to never join. And he stresses the dangers of rap music, which glorifies gangs and the use of drugs and alcohol.

The temptation to join gangs has also been strengthened by video games. They have sometimes made gang life attractive to teenagers by promoting violence, particularly against women and law enforcement. Such messages are often subliminal, but they make violence and criminality appear exciting, thereby encouraging a gang lifestyle.

Those who scoff at the link between playing violent games and delinquency should learn about research conducted at Iowa State University, which showed a definite connection. The results surprised Douglas Gentile, an associate psychology professor at the school who had studied the effects of exposure to video game violence and minor aggression such as hitting, teasing and name-calling. What he learned was that playing such games played a significant role in far more dangerous behavior.

"I didn't expect to see much of an effect when we got to serious delinquent and criminal behavior aggression because youth who commit that level of aggression have a lot of things going wrong for them," Gentile explained. "They often have a lot of risk factors and very few protective factors in their lives."

The results of the study were published in the April 2013 issue of *Youth Violence and Juvenile Justice*. It examined the video game exposure of 227 juvenile offenders in Pennsylvania that had averaged nearly nine serious acts of violence in the previous year, such as gang fighting, hitting a parent or attacking another person. And it showed that both the frequency of playing violent video games and the enjoyment of the activity were strongly linked to that delinquent and violent behavior. Though it was not the only cause for violent tendencies in youths, it was a definite risk factor.

An awareness of the effects of violent video games is important to those at the crossroads between gang membership and a healthy lifestyle. One should commit to playing non-violent video games, which can provide an immense challenge and enjoyment. But those who enjoy playing games associated with any level of violence should be fully aware of the risks and the fictional nature of the activity and not allow themselves to be affected by those games in their daily lives.

The same holds true for movies that depict or even promote gang violence. For decades, movies have placed a spotlight on gang warfare, but the majority have cast a negative light on the senseless tragedy associated with it. In more recent years, many films have become more graphic as they provide a more realistic representation of the violence and death linked to gang banging. Movies such as *South Central* and *Boyz in the Hood* have received critical acclaim for their realism.

Those considering gang membership would be wise to soak in the grittiest of films that provide truthful and detailed accounts of gang life. Unlike video games, which are fictional and do not offer a genuine representation, films that realistically depict gang warfare can scare one straight about its dangers. The more you know about gang violence and the threat of winding up dead or in jail, the more likely you are to make the decision to stay away.

Rap songs, video games, and movies have all proven to affect those making decisions about gang membership. It is critical to embrace the most realistic media representations and not those that glorify the violence associated with gangs. After all, realism is truth. And when one understands the truth about a gang lifestyle, the choice to reject it while remaining safe and healthy becomes easier to make. The right path is not to stop listening to music, playing video games, or going to movies. It is to understand the difference between realistic and unrealistic portrayals of gang life.

Perhaps you have dabbled in gang culture. You are at the crossroads. Studies have shown that you are not alone. One survey revealed that more than one-third of youths that had not been gang members had at least one as a friend or had worn gang colors. About 20 percent of the youths surveyed had flashed gang signs. Another survey showed that only 5 percent of ten thousand students in Florida claimed to be in gangs, but half of those who were not in gangs still had engaged in gang-related activities such as wearing gang colors on purpose or using drugs or alcohol with gang members. While it would be best to distance yourself from any affiliation with gangs, it's critical that you understand the dangers of joining and make a conscious effort to embrace a healthier lifestyle.

BEING HONEST WITH YOURSELF

It's also important that you not only become aware of the risk factors for gang membership, but recognize as well how you fit in. One must be honest when assessing his or her own vulnerabilities. They don't include only individual issues. School, family, peers, and community all play a role in influencing decisions in regard to gang membership.

Low academic achievement and poorly functioning and unsafe schools have been identified as two significant risk factors. Studies have shown that future gang members performed poorly in elementary school and

One should always opt for a healthy, safe existence rather than the dangers and criminality associated with gang life.

displayed a lack of commitment to education. They were often suspended or even expelled from school, which removed them from adult supervision and exposed them to opportunities for delinquent behavior. Those who feel vulnerable or bullied at school are also more likely candidates to join gangs.

Several family issues increase risk factors as well, including one-parent homes with other adults under the same roof or families in a cycle of poverty. Parents who grew up poor with little education and have been saddled with a low socioeconomic status throughout their lives are far more likely to raise children who will join a gang. They're also more prone to violence in their rearing of children, which their offspring often carry over into gang life.

One study linked association with peers who engage in delinquency as the strongest risk factor for gang membership, particularly for boys. Even those who hang around non-delinquents who still display an aggressiveness and violent tendencies are more likely to join gangs. Another peer-related risk factor is unpopularity. Those who feel rebuffed by their peers are stronger candidates for gang membership. They are desperate for friendship in any form, and their anger and frustration over rejection by others leads them into the gang trap.

Economically struggling communities or neighborhoods are more likely to produce gangs as well. They tend to be plagued by them. Youths in poor and dangerous areas often seek protection through gangs. The availability of substances and guns can draw in disadvantaged youths. They feel the need to make money through drug sales or other criminal activity. Studies have shown that exposure to firearm violence approximately doubles the probability that an adolescent will carry out serious violence over the next two years.

By that time, individual risk factors have played out in a dangerous way. Children involved in delinquency, violence, and drug use at an early age are at a higher risk for gang membership than others. Studies have also shown that adolescents dealing with mental health issues are more likely to join gangs, as are those who grew up as victims of violence and aggression. Various issues regarding behavior and personality have been associated with future gang members. Those with a penchant for aggressiveness and recklessness are strong candidates. So are those who prove themselves to be manipulative, superficial, irresponsible, or cold-hearted.

The individuals with the greatest number of risk factors are the most likely to join gangs. One study revealed that children with seven or more risk factor indicators were thirteen times more likely to join a gang than those with zero or one. But the study provided hope as well. Studies by the National Gang Center indicated that less than one-third of those with a large number of risk factors become gang members. Just over half of all gang members experienced eleven or more risk factors.

The person you see in the mirror ultimately makes the final decision on gang membership.

Risk factors don't definitively cause youths to join gangs, they only increase the probability. The more you know about risk factors and the dangers of gang life, the more of an informed judgment you can make. Perhaps you will know why some lose the battle of temptation and join gangs. And hopefully you will have learned that making the same call can lead to nothing but misery, physical and emotional harm, and even death.

What do you see when you look in the mirror? Self-respect is a key to happiness—and joining a gang is a sure way to lose your self-respect.

MYTHS AND FACTS

MYTH

My gang will protect me from bullies and other gang members.

FACT

Being in a gang greatly increases your chances of being a target of a rival gang member, which makes you much more likely to be injured or killed if you are in a gang.

MYTH

I will make a lot of money if I am in a gang.

FACT

Most people make very little money being a part of a gang. Those that do most often end up in jail. As the National Counter Street Gang Intelligence Center notes, getting a job and an education are far safer and more lucrative money-making ventures.

MYTH

My gang will be just like a family.

FACT

Real families don't force their offspring or siblings to commit crimes to get respect and love. Real families accept and love you unconditionally.

CHAPTER 2

Happy and contented people are rarely motivated to join gangs. Those that enjoy healthy relationships with family and friends, embrace education and school activities, and look forward to making positive contributions to society are not candidates for gang membership. Life is good for them.

Only the dissatisfied feel the need to take such a drastic and harmful step. Many come from broken homes or dysfunctional families. Perhaps they have suffered physical, sexual, or mental abuse. The majority live in poor neighborhoods that are struggling with underperforming schools, high crime rates, and fewer opportunities for fulfilling social relationships.

Young people join gangs for a myriad of reasons. The most common are alienation from social institutions such as family and school. When those links are broken, teenagers tend to stray emotionally and physically. They're predisposed to antisocial behavior and delinquency. They're more easily tempted by the use of alcohol and drugs, precocious sexual behavior, and violent crime. They're vulnerable to peer pressure. They seek strong bonds lacking in their lives. They're looking for fun and a sense of family that they can't find elsewhere. They yearn to make fast money through the sale of drugs or robbery rather than the tedious, low-paying jobs commonly accepted by teenagers.

A relationship with a friend or family member already in a gang can tip the scales in a negative way. Those who perceive that people they know are thriving in gang life tend to follow in their footsteps. A romantic interest with a gang member might also motivate one to join. But though there might be a dozen or more motivations for gang membership, there's one common denominator, which is dissatisfaction with one or

Running from rival gang members and the law often lands gang members in filthy areas of town such as this.

Handcuffs and jail time are sad realities for gang bangers, who usually try unsuccessfully to stay one step ahead of the law.

more important aspect of life, as noted by the National Crime Prevention Council.

Yet every perceived reason for joining a gang brings false hope and promises. Those suffering from such negativity seek a quick fix by joining a gang. Among the attractions is the ability to earn more money in the short term. That can be a powerful force, especially for those in poor neighborhoods plagued by limited employment opportunities. But embracing a gang for financial rewards is fraught with danger. Every money-making scheme, such as selling drugs, burglarizing homes, stealing cars, or robbing stores, is illegal. All can lead to arrest and prison sentences.

BIGGER BUCKS, SMALLER GANGS?

A strong push for a higher minimum wage for jobs has became a hotly debated topic. Bernie Sanders, who ran a presidential campaign as a Democrat in 2016, offered that it should be doubled to $15 an hour. Some states had already raised their minimum wages significantly.

Many believe such a move would reduce gang violence because gang members could earn far more money in legitimate jobs than they could have in the past while staying safe. Among the cities supporters felt such a wage hike could help was Chicago, which had been the most violent in the country. The huge Illinois city experienced more than five hundred homicides, mostly gang related, in 2012 alone.

One 2013 report claimed a distinct connection between violent crime, low wages, and economic inequality in Chicago. Previous research showed that the majority of violent crime in Chicago could be tied to downward trends in income. The National Bureau of Economic Research reported a 20 percent drop in wages led to a 12 to 18 percent increase in youth crime. And the number of Chicago workers earning just $12 an hour or less had increased by 30 percent over the previous decade.

The report also stated that nearly 90 percent of all murders and violent crimes in Chicago had been committed in areas where wages were lowest and poverty levels were highest.

The battle over drug money by rival gangs is often the centerpiece of gang activity. It's the reason that many gang bangers end up dead. You must weigh the likelihood of a jail term or the danger of getting murdered against the possibility of making money through illegal acts. And you should therefore ask yourself if it's not far better for your life to seek out a job that brings steady income, a sense of pride in yourself, the safety of living as a law-abiding citizen, and the work ethic needed to embark on a healthy and productive path in life.

DON'T FOOL YOURSELF

The attraction of family is also a false one. You should ask yourself if your fellow gang members really care about you as a brother or sister. After all, a brother or sister wouldn't ask you to put your life and freedom at risk through dangerous and illegal activities. A family seeks to bring out the best in one another. It yearns to place its members on a positive and healthy path in life. If your family doesn't fit that description, that doesn't mean your fellow gang members would be any better. Gang members target you only for what you can bring to them. They see strength in numbers. And they don't care about your physical or emotional well-being.

You might also perceive gang membership as a form of protection from violence. It's quite the opposite. Gang warfare is notorious for escalation and revenge. You must ask yourself why so many gang members wind up in hospitals or morgues. For every gang there are many rival gangs. You require protection only from rival gangs when you are in a gang.

Gang members have no reason to target you if you are no threat to them. Teenagers quite often think with their emotions instead of their brains. Only through logic can one make healthy decisions. Perceived threats in your life can be better handled through intervention from those trained to help, such as school counselors and law enforcement officials. Getting gangs involved is a dangerous and potentially lethal step.

Those who opt for gang membership to join a friend, relative, or romantic interest are not only being

Nobody is safe when rival gangs battle over turf or money from illegal activities—fights can lead to severe injuries or even death.

GIRLS IN GANGS

Studies have produced some interesting facts about the prevalence of females in American gangs. The numbers have held steady, but the demographics vary by the types of communities in which they live.

Every study from 1998 to 2010 revealed that only 6 to 8 percent of all gang members in the United States were female. But nearly one-quarter of the law enforcement agencies did not provide information about female gang population. That leads to the belief that the agencies consider girl gang members to be a significantly lesser issue. Of the agencies, 15 percent reported no female gang activity.

The difference is that gangs in large cities, where the problem is more pervasive, have a far smaller percentage of female members. A 2009 study showed that only 23 percent of gangs in large cities include females. But smaller cities, suburban counties, and rural areas all reported that more than 40 percent of their gangs had females in them. In fact, such was the case in nearly half of all rural gangs.

Rural counties also were the only demographic in which most of their gang members were eighteen years old or younger. The lowest proportion of juvenile members were in large cities, where about two-thirds of gang members are older than eighteen.

Gang life can be lonely and sad as fellow gang members prove that they are not the best of friends.

foolish, but are also enabling a negative role in their lives. You would be strengthening the hold of the gang on those you love. You would be justifying their decision to join by joining it yourself, thereby placing them in greater danger of all the pitfalls that gang membership brings. If you want them to be part of your life, a far more positive tactic is to try convincing those close to you to get out of the gang. You will not only earn their respect and admiration, but they will understand that you truly care about them.

Some female adolescents become attracted to gangs because their friends or boyfriends have joined. Though they're not generally recognized as members by the male gang population, they're integrated into the group. Research by James C. Howell in "Gang Prevention: an Overview of Research and Programs" showed that they begin hanging out with the gang before the age of twelve. About four in five girls in the study later reported they had a male friend or boyfriend in the gang they joined. The association leads them into delinquent behavior and criminal activity.

Another perceived attraction for some to join gangs is simply fun. However, there's a difference between excitement and fun. Robbing a store, stealing a car, or brawling with a rival gang are only exciting because they're dangerous. There's nothing fun about spending your days and nights knowing that you can be killed or seriously injured at any time. There's nothing fun about getting arrested for the illegal deeds inherent in gang life and spending months or years in jail. There's nothing fun about fighting with guns and knives over turf or drug money. Gang activities that threaten freedom and life are not fun.

Fun is tied to emotional fulfillment, the notion of enjoying a positive experience, whether you are alone or with friends and family members. The knowledge that you are endangering your life or, at best, placing yourself on a path to nowhere as a gang member, precludes any possibility of having fun.

It has been said that when life gives you lemons, make lemonade. That means life is what you make of it and that hurdles can be cleared. The expression is meaningful to those considering gang membership because of their frustrations over various aspects of their lives. History is replete with stories of those who have overcome hardship to not only live above the law, but also be productive and make a positive impact on the world.

MAKING SOMETHING SWEET FROM SOMETHING SOUR

One reason you might be tempted to join a gang is dissatisfaction with school. But you should work to make lemonade out of those sour lemons. School is what you make of it. Those who are open to various educational and social resources rather than dismissing school as a waste of time are happier in the short term and beyond. Education is exploration. Knowledge is power. Gangs don't allow you to grow mentally.

Though schools are working to limit or eliminate gangs operating under their roofs, studies have shown that students boast a greater awareness than administrators in regard to gang activity in their schools. Research concluded in 2009 revealed that many educators believe that the problem exists only in the community and not on their campuses. Only 5 percent of principles surveyed reported a gang presence in their schools, but more than one-third of them cited gangs in the streets. Students, however, have an awareness of gang symbols, hand gestures, clothing, and gang lingo, and are far more adept at spotting gang members. Teachers and administrators might not recognize gang activity when they see it.

Some might also shy away from acknowledging a gang problem at their school because it could be perceived as an admission of failure and cause parents to remove students from their schools. Counselors, teachers, and administrators can be wonderful resources to discuss your specific problem in regard to gangs. Sharon Issurdatt notes in her study "Gangs: A Growing Problem in Schools" that it's up to you to recognize what is happening with gangs at your school and to gain a positive educational and social experience by steadfastly avoiding gang activity.

One way to do that is to avoid drugs. Many gang killings have been motivated by drug money. But you should also know that some youths join gangs as a way of deepening their relationships with the drug culture, as well as the drinking of alcohol. Studies from the Institute of Public Health have shown that gang members are significantly more likely than others to have begun drinking at an early age and to have become heavy drinkers. They're also more likely to have become involved in heavy drug use. Gang membership dramatically shifts one's peer group. You make a conscious effort to hang out with alcohol and drug users who are often addicts when you join a gang. This just adds to the number of aspects of gang membership that could prove to be destructive to your life.

Your energy instead should be geared toward finding and remaining on a positive path. Every motivation for gang membership also has healthy alternatives. Whether it's the need for money or friendship or protection or simply a desire to enjoy life, opportunities abound. Self-worth should be attained through the knowledge that you are forging a rewarding path to the future, not by risking your life for false promises.

EXPLORING YOUR POSITIVE SIDE

A positive self-image is perhaps the most essential attribute anyone can attain. How others see you is perception. That is important. But what you see in yourself when judging honestly is reality, and that is more significant. The relatively new expression that "perception is reality" is flawed. People are often misjudged. What a person sees when he or she looks in the mirror reflects a self-image that can determine success or failure in life.

Those who believe that gang membership and activity will increase self-respect are fooling themselves. Every challenge in life that can motivate a person to join a gang can be countered by positive action. If you want to make money, there are legal and legitimate options. If you seek emotional and physical security, possibilities abound in trusted personal relationships, school, and community. If you are looking for fun and excitement, you need not look any farther than your own interests. And if you desire to find friends or a romantic relationship through gang membership, you are simply looking in the wrong place.

You are a unique person. A sense of individuality is critical in the pursuit of happiness. Joining a gang is a negative expression of conformity. You should explore group activities that allow you to make friends and be a part of a larger community, yet provide the freedom to maintain that feeling of uniqueness that makes you special.

Earning fast and easy money is a perceived benefit of gang membership. No illegal means of making money is fast and easy, and every one of them, including robbery, prostitution, or drug sales, can result in imprisonment or even death. Seeking out and finding a job is a far safer, more gratifying and potentially career-boosting alternative. Working at a fast-food restaurant or local store might not pique your personal interests, but it's steady income. That certainly beats putting your life on the line in a gang.

Creativity in the working world is the best way to strengthen your self-image. You should explore your interests and seek out jobs or even create your own work which allows you to foster that interest. Perhaps you enjoy films. Then try to find a job at a movie theater. If you like sports, then seek out employment at a ballpark or sports-wear store. Those who love animals should find out if there's a job opening at a pet shop or vet's office.

There are no guarantees that you will find a match. Perhaps the business to which you apply has no opening at that moment. But at least you will receive the self-satisfaction of having tried your best. And you will know where to look in the future. Don't give up after one

One should explore and enjoy his or her individuality rather than conform by joining a gang.

attempt. Let employers know that you are very interested in working for them. They will be flattered and will keep you in mind when an opening does arise.

GO FOR IT!

Another option that will strengthen your self-image and provide the enjoyment that might not be available in more menial jobs is to start your own business. This will again give you an opportunity to explore your passions. Perhaps you are talented and versed enough in an activity to provide lessons to others. Or maybe you possess the ability to create artwork for sale. Many teens launch their own landscaping businesses. Such endeavors will likely not earn you the amount of money as steady employment working for a business, but they can make you rich in regard to self-respect and independence while blazing a trail for a future career. The more you work at a craft, the better you will get and the closer you will be to reaching a professional level.

The same holds true in your personal life. Those that perceive gang membership as a pathway to friendships and a sense of family that perhaps were lacking in their lives are in for a rude awakening.

Many healthier and emotionally fulfilling options exist. One is to befriend acquaintances at school or in the neighborhood who are embracing positive lifestyles. Perhaps you know someone that partakes in an activity you would like to try. Or you can simply ask if he or she would simply like to hang out. Study together, see a movie, go bowling, or play miniature golf. Have fun with your new friend. Do something that will be make you feel good about yourself. Most people embrace an opportunity to make new friends. They will probably be flattered that you showed an interest.

Getting a job brings self-respect and a far safer way of making money than gang banging.

Schools and communities offer many positive outlets for youths seeking to make the most of their free time.

Programs for teenagers abound. The National Gang Center notes that the Boys and Girls Clubs of America offer opportunities to remain out of gangs while enjoying a myriad of activities.

Their Gang Prevention Through Targeted Outreach program works to intervene with at-risk youths. The Boys and Girls Clubs offer programs based on individual interests and needs. The gang prevention program recruits teenagers, but you are certainly welcome to take the initiative and join. Programs are offered in five core areas: character and leadership development, education and career development, health and life skills, the arts, and sports, fitness, and recreation. Research has shown that those participating are less likely to have contact with the juvenile court system, exhibit delinquent behaviors, and wear gang colors. They have also improved peer and family relationships, as well as school performance.

THE OPRAH WINFREY STORY

Millions of Americans over the years have overcome poverty to gain fame and fortune. They have proved that though growing up poor creates greater obstacles to success, conviction, and confidence can bring triumph in life.

Among the greatest of all American success stories is legendary talk show host and actress Oprah Winfrey, who is the daughter of an unwed teenage mother from rural Mississippi. Winfrey not only conquered poverty, but also sexual abuse and her own teenage pregnancy to become one of the most influential celebrities ever.

Winfrey showed her grit by landing a job at a local television station in high school. She then recevied a scholarship to Tennessee State University before finding work as a news anchor in Baltimore and Nashville. She eventually became a talk show host in Chicago, where she transformed her station from one of the lowest-rated to the highest-rated in the city.

Her show later became a national phenomenon as millions of Americans embraced her positive outlook and interviewing style. Her incredible success allowed her to create her own television network. She also gained a level of success as an actress in such movies as *The Color Purple*, *The Butler*, and *Selma*.

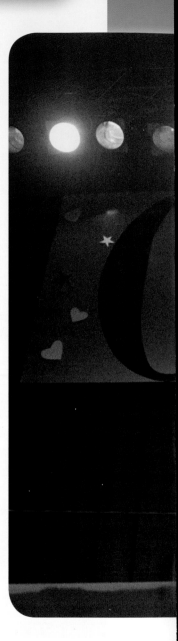

Multi-talented superstar Oprah Winfrey became a tremendously positive role model for young people after overcoming a difficult childhood.

The National Association of Police runs a program via the Police Athletic/Activity League. The organization seeks to gain the respect and appreciation of young people for law enforcement through healthy relationships. It offers more than one hundred activities, some of which are sure to pique the interest of any teenager. Included are sports as varied as football, rock climbing, horseback riding, arts and crafts, science, hip-hop, journalism, theater, graphic arts, and cheerleading. The Police Athletic/Activity League also offers practical educational programs that can help you in school and plan your future, such as career instruction, student council, college prep, life skills, tutoring, and homework help.

Programs such as these serve three primary purposes. They provide positive outlets for time and energy, open pathways to future professional success, and offer opportunities to make new friends. School activities can do the same, as well as give another example of why school is what you make of it. Joining a sports team or after-school club will prove far more fulfilling than hanging out with a gang both emotionally and—in the case of athletics—physically. It also gives you a chance to get to know yourself better by working to select an activity that you will embrace.

REPAIRING HOME DAMAGE

You can also take steps to repair an unsatisfying family life or make the most of a broken home, both of which have been proven to push youths into gangs. Whether it's a father or mother or brother or sister or even a care-taker, it's important that you make your feelings known. Letting a family member know that you want to improve your relationship plants the seed for success. Tell a parent that you yearn for love and affection. An important role for parents is to discipline their kids and monitor personal relationships so they don't fall in with the wrong crowd. If you are indeed working to avoid the temptation of joining a gang, you would be wise to ask for help from any trusted adult family member. Older siblings can also give valuable assistance, particularly since they have likely gone through the same experiences and are aware of the lure of gang membership.

Joining a gang can sometimes be a rash decision based on sudden urges or dissatisfaction that reaches a critical stage. It's important that you refuse to give in to negative impulses. Hobbies that you can partake in on your own are always helpful alternatives to alleviating your problems and concerns. Ride your bike through the neighborhood or in a local park. Organize a game of basketball.

Take a walk or jog. Go somewhere fun like a movie or bowling alley. Go shopping and buy yourself something you have always wanted. Spur-of-the-moment activities not only provide a diversion, but they reinforce a needed belief that healthy activities are more enjoyable and fulfilling than the illegal and dangerous ones pursued by gang members.

Poor classroom performance and habits often motivate youths to join gangs. School seems meaningless to

some, but one should understand that it's not just an institution of learning. School also allows students to lay the foundation for habits and a work ethic that will prove vital to future success in both their professional and personal lives. You can't fully appreciate the self-satisfaction inherent in performing well in school until that has been achieved, and that can't be achieved until you summon up the motivation.

Some teenagers tend to dismiss this notion. They perceive school as uncool. They don't see school as a means to both current and future happiness and contentment. You can be different, but it takes a commitment. Attend all your classes. Listen to your teacher. Ask him or her questions if you are struggling. Take notes. Do your homework. Study for your tests. Put your heart and soul into your schoolwork, and you will feel proud of yourself. You will also feel empowered, and self-empowerment is a key component to shunning gangs. Those who believe in themselves don't need others to massage their egos and justify their worth.

Resources within the school and community can provide help. But it's you that must take the initiative. Treat yourself as someone important—because you are.

Participating in sports such as basketball is a healthier and safer way to spend free time than running around with a gang.

CHAPTER 4

WHAT NOT TO DO

Perceived gang pressure can make you feel trapped. You might feel threatened or at least pressured to join. But the power gained from knowledge should allay those fears. Research has shown conclusively that gang membership is driven by individual decisions to join based on personal relationships, promises of fast money, protection, fun, and excitement. James C. Howell concludes that gangs rarely pressure others to join. They lure you in with false hopes instead.

Yet that fear can still remain. You understand that gang bangers can be dangerous. You understand that they often have weapons. You understand that there's strength in numbers and that they want you. Michelle Arciaga Young's 2013 study of leaving gangs found that the "just say no" alternative works. Even more important to know is that if you have already joined a gang, those who decide to leave nearly always do without repercussion.

Fear can be a powerful motivating emotion. Some teenagers feel such pressure in their lives that they simply run away. That is a dangerous response. It's ironic but true that fleeing would place you in greater danger of gang violence. Homeless teenagers are far more likely to be victims of crime and sexual abuse, sometimes from the very gang members they're seeking to avoid. Studies done by the US National Library of Medicine and the National Institute for Health have shown that runaways have significantly higher rates of depression, as well as alcohol and drug abuse. They're far more prone to suicidal thoughts and action. Girls who flee are more likely to become pregnant.

Other means of escape should also be avoided. Many turn to alcohol or drugs as a way to leave their emotional struggles behind. It's unhealthy and potentially dangerous to abuse alcohol and drugs, and you must also realize that they will only add to your problems. Even if they allow you to temporarily forget the issues you are dealing with—and they probably won't— you will be facing the same dilemma when the booze or drugs wear off. It's more likely, however, that they will cause you to wallow in your misery even more. Substance abuse can also play a significant role when deciding to join a gang. Overall, getting drunk or stoned simply wastes time in your search for happiness and fulfillment and can plant the seeds for addiction that can haunt you for a lifetime.

You should avoid any confusion about gang membership. Sitting on the fence might motivate you to take an unsafe leap of faith. You might rationalize and decide to join a gang as a short-term experiment to see if you enjoy the experience. But though statistics show

Money made through illegal gang activities brings nothing but fear of landing in jail or even death.

that most former gang members left without incident, it remains a risk. Professor Mike Carlie of sociology and criminology at Missouri State University researched the subject and wrote a book about it titled *Into the Abyss: A Personal Journey Into the World of Street Gangs*. The following excerpt tells you all you need to know about the potential danger of leaving a gang:

> A juvenile officer...told me a story about a local gang member who wanted to get out of his gang. "I got a call from a client named Fernando," she said, "who told me he needed help. He was frightened... he didn't want to be in the gang anymore." As far as the officer

was concerned, "He was in too far. I didn't think he could get out. He actually wanted me to lock him up so that he'd stay out of trouble."

The officer told her client that she couldn't do that, so he broke into a car, stole some things, assaulted his parents and another youth then fled. "He wanted to get locked up…he tried doing some things he could get locked up for." Another of her gang clients told her "I'm going to kill him," referring to the young man who wanted to leave the gang. "He can't leave."

SHORT STAYS, TOUGH DEPARTURES

Leaving a gang can indeed be dangerous. One study in Carlie's book surveyed three gang-infested neighborhoods in Washington, DC, and showed that membership generally lasted between one or two years. But those who sought to leave were sometimes beaten up in order to receive permission. Many who were luckier simply stopped hanging out with the gang and pursued new interests. Others were threatened by rival gangs, which they believed forced them to remain in their current gangs for protection. Another issue was that their gang affiliation followed some into the working world. They were labeled as a risk by employers

Law-enforcement officials are allies to those seeking to stay out of gangs or escape gangs they might have joined.

and found it difficult to find a job. That, in turn, caused them to stay in or rejoin a gang.

The book also featured the results of interviews with several youths who reported they had to leave their hometowns to escape the gangs they had joined. Even that did not solve their problem. Sometimes they were followed by gang members or felt threatened by affiliated gang members in the area in which they moved. They feared that they would be tracked down and harmed. There seemed to be no escape.

Another excerpt relayed a story told by a gang enforcement officer about young men seeking to escape a gang. They're placed in an old refrigerator laid on the ground. The door is shut and other gang members fire guns into it. If he survives, he is out. If he is killed, he is out forever. Either way, he is out of the gang.

The lesson here is that you shouldn't dip your toes in the water. Don't give in to your curiosity about gang life. If you already have joined a gang and wish to leave, seek the help of law enforcement officials and let them know you feel threatened.

An experiment with gangs can prove fatal. So can seeking a violent way out. You might be tempted to engage in battle against those you believe are bullying you into a joining a gang. However, it takes far more will power to avoid that temptation than it does to follow through with it. A mature person who values his or her future and life itself gathers the inner strength to remain uninvolved in the first place. The fact that gangs lure members through perceived benefits rather than force you to join should serve as a constant reminder that it's best to just say no. You must also remind yourself of the myriad of helpful resources available among family and friends, at school, and in the community. Make the most of them.

NO BRAWLS, NO GUNS

Confrontation is never the answer. Neither is appeasing gang members. One might be tempted to wear the clothing or colors, flash the symbols used by gang members, or just hang out with them as a way to show empathy without joining. But that approach could prove dangerous. If you look like a gang member or are seen with them, you could be mistaken by a rival gang as a member and victimized by violent behavior.

The Violence Prevention Institute stresses that it's especially important you don't carry a gun or other weapon. They don't make you safer. They tend to escalate conflicts and increase the chances you will be seriously injured or even killed. Those who feel threatened should find a trusted adult to discuss their fears or contact school officials or a police officer. They should also take precautions against being alone. One is far less likely to be targeted in a group.

That can best be accomplished by maintaining a positive social and educational life. Loneliness can lead to gang membership. Some struggling youth become desperate enough to drop out of school. That not only serves to block their pathway to a productive and

THE WATTS TRUCE

One of the strongest examples of what the most hardened gang members can accomplish when they put down their guns and come together was achieved in the Watts section of Los Angeles in 1992. The area had been the center of a fierce and deadly battle for three decades between two rival gangs, the Bloods and the Crips, in which hundreds had been killed.

The Bloods wore red. The Crips wore blue. And if a member of one gang found himself in the territory of the other, he was often gunned down. The two gangs battled over turf and drug money while engaging in many other illegal and dangerous activities.

A former gang member named Aqeela Sherrills decided to take action. He worked to bring the gang members together. He organized meetings, some of which were extremely tense. But he eventually brokered a truce between Bloods and Crips that resulted in 44 percent fewer homicides in the city in just one year, as reported by the BBC in April 2015.

Though gang activity remains a major problem in Los Angeles, the crime and homicide rates have continued to decline. Citydata.com revealed that the murder rate there has fallen about 60 percent from 2002 to 2013. Other crimes, such as robberies, assaults, and car thefts, also dropped drastically during that time.

An attempt to lessen violence between the Crips and Bloods of Los Angeles proved successful, but it did not end gang activity.

fulfilling future, but it creates a time vacuum that some fill by joining a gang. They lose touch with friends and classmates who had been positive influences in their lives. They lose associations with after-school clubs or sports teams that provided healthy diversions.

Though it's generally best to complete your high school education and pursue a college degree if financially possible, it's understandable if you leave school in favor of a job to help support your family. One should take pride in doing the right thing for one's family. Time spent on the job earning a living legally is far more productive and emotionally stabilizing than seeking to make money in a gang robbing, stealing, and selling drugs. And one can always complete their education later in life. Money earned on the job can even be saved toward a college education in which you can pursue a professional dream.

Those who don't distance themselves from gangs keep open the possibility of joining. Any affiliation can be dangerous, whether it's hanging out with gang members, flashing their signs, or wearing their colors. You need not show disrespect or threaten violence against gang members to make known your intention to remain independent. But you shouldn't give those trying to lure you into a gang any indication that you are interested. The most effective way to achieve that is to take every positive step to ensure a healthy and rewarding lifestyle while using all the resources available to you to remain gang-free.

1. How do I know that I'm being targeted by a gang?

2. How often does gang violence occur in schools?

3. Should I ask former gang members for advice on how to stay out?

4. Who role do most females serve in gangs?

5. Should I just ignore requests to join a gang or do I need to verbally say no?

6. What is the safest way to get a friend or family member out of a gang?

7. Do all gangs engage in illegal activity?

8. What community programs work best for someone trying to stay out of a gang?

9. Is it important to keep my anti-gang activities secret from gang members?

10. Should I avoid wearing gang colors even if I am not in a gang?

CHAPTER 5

FRIENDS AND FAMILY WANT TO HELP

Only you can keep yourself out of gangs. But your pride shouldn't get in the way if you find yourself fighting temptation. You should be open to enlisting the assistance of others.

Wise youths use wise mentors to help them make wise decisions. Much thought should enter into choosing those best suited to provide advice and direction. Several things should factor into what is a very important step.

Ask yourself who you can trust to keep your thoughts and concerns confidential. You will be sharing concerns with someone about making life-altering decisions. What is discussed with that person is not for the ears of others, particularly those of gang members trying to lure you in.

One should not be afraid to elicit the help of family members in fighting the urge to join a gang.

Ask yourself who is most well-versed on the subject. Those with gang experience or intimate knowledge of gang life are far better qualified to advise you than those with little or no familiarity with gangs.

Ask yourself who among your friends and family members cares the most about your welfare. Those with only a passing interest might not offer well-thought-out advice from the heart. However, those close to you emotionally will put everything they have into nudging you along the path to freedom from gangs or out of the gang if you have already joined.

Keep in mind, however, that you are not weighing alternatives. You are not learning perceived pros and cons of joining a gang or remaining in one. You should have already made the decision to stay out of gangs or leave the one you have joined. There's no need to speak with a gang member to get his or her side about the so-called benefits of gang life. You are seeking out those who can help push you in the right direction and allow you to live your life in a manner that will keep temptation away. You are looking for those who can offer advice that will provide you with a sense of positivity.

Some youths must repair broken relationships with family members before seeking their aid. Many gang members are products of dysfunctional or broken homes. A cycle of poverty and lawlessness, particularly among inner-city communities, often results in sons following fathers into gang life and jail. If your family falls into that category, you should make a vow to

One anti-gang initiative in which you can involve yourself is the Neighborhood Watch, which is among the oldest crime prevention programs in the United States. Its official literature states that its roots can be traced back to the colonial days, when night watchmen patrolled the streets. In contemporary times, it began in the 1970s to reduce incidents of home burglaries. Soon, it evolved into a program that organized local watch groups who encouraged citizens to keep an eye out for various types of neighborhood crime. It became quite proactive in more recent years.

An analysis by the US Department of Justice in 2008 revealed that the Neighborhood Watch program had a positive effect on crime. The studies examined the relationship between crime reduction and citizen policing programs between 1977 and 1994, about half of which were in the United States and the other half mainly in the United Kingdom, plus one in Canada. The result was that there was an average of a 16 percent reduction in crime in those areas. Still, it claimed that some programs worked far better than others.

KEEPING AN EYE ON THE NEIGHBORHOOD

break that cycle. Parents or siblings who understand what you are going through can empathize and provide you with advice based on their own experiences.

GETTING HELP FROM MOM AND POP

Let your parents know that you welcome their help, especially if are wavering in your commitment to stay out of gangs. The American Academy of Child and Adolescent Psychiatry lists a number of ways parents can help their kids remain on a positive path. Included are closely monitoring where they are and what they're doing, involving them in activities and after-school programs such as sports, clubs, community organizations and

Positive, open relationships between teenagers and their parents are critical to success in keeping kids out of gangs.

religious groups, and meeting their friends.

Parents can also prevent at-risk adolescents from wearing, writing, or gesturing gang-related graffiti, signs, or symbols. They can discuss with their offspring gang involvement and criminal behavior and remind them that they can wind up injured, in jail, or even dead.

Perhaps you feel strongly enough about your ability to monitor yourself that such help from parents and siblings is unnecessary. However, too little adult supervision has been cited as one reason youths join gangs. There's strength in numbers. The more trusted and caring people you can find invested in your well-being, the safer

Intervention programs between schools and law enforcement can prove to be a valuable weapon against gang activity.

you will be. You don't want to be alone in your conviction to stay out of gangs, especially when gang members are working to lure you in.

Nobody wants to fight solo. That is why you should play a role at your school. Learn more about what your school is doing in the battle against gangs. Research has shown that many administrators lack awareness of gang activity in their schools. They might be unaware of the warning signs, such as the wearing of gang colors and flashing of gang signs or gang-related graffiti on the walls. You don't need to make your contributions to an anti-gang drive known to gang members. You don't need to "fink" on any of them. You can simply and privately let those in charge know that they have a gang problem while making them aware of the evidence.

You can also inform school administrators of programs that could help lessen the effect of gangs on schools and their students. One that is particularly popular and that has gained a level of success at middle schools is the Gang Resistance Education and Training (GREAT) Program. GREAT has worked to build trust both nationally and internationally between students and law enforcement for more than three decades. It seeks to eliminate delinquency, youth violence, and gang membership in schools and in the community.

The program allows law enforcement officials to enter the classroom for thirteen lessons to speak with middle school students and six more in elementary schools.

Though gangs have recruited youths at younger ages, the instruction is intended to nip the problem in the bud before those students become prime targets. More than thirteen thousand sworn police officers from around the United States and Central American countries, where gang problems have also proliferated, have delivered lessons to more than six million students.

ISN'T THAT GREAT?

The work of GREAT has fostered a stronger relationship between the police and teens whose earned respect can go a long way in keeping them out of gangs. The program has partnered with such national organizations as the Boys and Girls Clubs and the Police Athletic/Activities League to encourage a strong collaboration between schools, parents, law enforcement, and the communities they serve.

The difference between GREAT and other programs is that it seeks to stop gang membership before it starts rather than targeting youths after they join. And though independent studies from the National Institute of Justice and the *Journal of School Violence* have shown mixed results, they have indicated that GREAT has had positive effects on the attitudes and delinquency risk factors of adolescents. Students reported more respectful attitudes toward police, less positive attitudes about gangs, more frequent use of refusal skills, greater resistance to peer pressure, and lower rates of gang membership. You can make a difference at your school by researching GREAT and other anti-gang programs and bringing awareness about them to your administration.

Your relationship with your school is a two-way street. You can help in the fight against gangs, but teachers, coaches, counselors, and administrators can also help you in your quest to stay out of gangs or leave one you have joined. Those you seek out don't need to know the inner-workings of gang life. They must simply advise and discuss with you the best path to take toward a positive outcome. School officials, counselors

Exploring one's positive side through activities such as dancing provides healthy outlets and no desire to join a gang.

in particular, are trained to suggest and implement appropriate plans that can keep you headed in the right direction both inside and outside their institutions.

Perhaps you need help in the classroom and with your work ethic. Counselors understand reasons for student apathy in education and will work with you to create an interest in particular subjects. Somewhere inside of you is a curious person who can embrace education, but who might also need an attitude adjustment and a belief that you are working through school to seek happiness and fulfillment. Your counselors, as well as trusted teachers and administrators, are trained to help. Their work can strengthen your level of self-respect, which, in turn, can eliminate in your mind any thoughts of joining a gang. After all, low self-esteem is one primary factor in youths becoming gang members.

You should also be mindful that the school experience extends beyond the classroom. Perhaps you are well-suited for a sports team, music or arts program, or club activity that can raise your self-esteem and provide a positive experience mentally, physically, and emotionally.

Most schools offer a myriad of possibilities. Ask yourself which interests you the most. Ask yourself which would benefit you in the future. Some after-school activities are suited to help students on a path to a career. Staying busy, especially doing something positive and legal that you enjoy, is a surefire way to keep you out of gangs.

There are other ways as well, involving community programs. It's gratifying and important to make yourself part of the bigger anti-gang picture. You can be a vital piece in the machinery that seeks to keep gangs out of your neighborhood.

CHAPTER 6

HELPING OTHERS, HELPING YOURSELF

The increase in gang violence in recent decades and resulting media attention have given birth to many community programs to combat the problem. Most of them work to turn gang members into responsible citizens, which is certainly a worthy endeavor. But others couple that purpose with initiatives to help youths help themselves before they take that dangerous step.

Among them is Amer-I-Can, which was launched by football legend Jim Brown in the late 1980s.

His program works to maximize the academic potential of at-risk kids and raise their behavioral performance to acceptable society standards. It seeks to give hope to kids through life management skills and training that focuses on improving attitude and self-esteem. Amer-I-Can convinces youths through repetition of positive behavior that their goals in life can be achieved and that they control their own destinies.

Football legend Jim Brown and his Amer-I-Can program have helped many youths stay out of gangs.

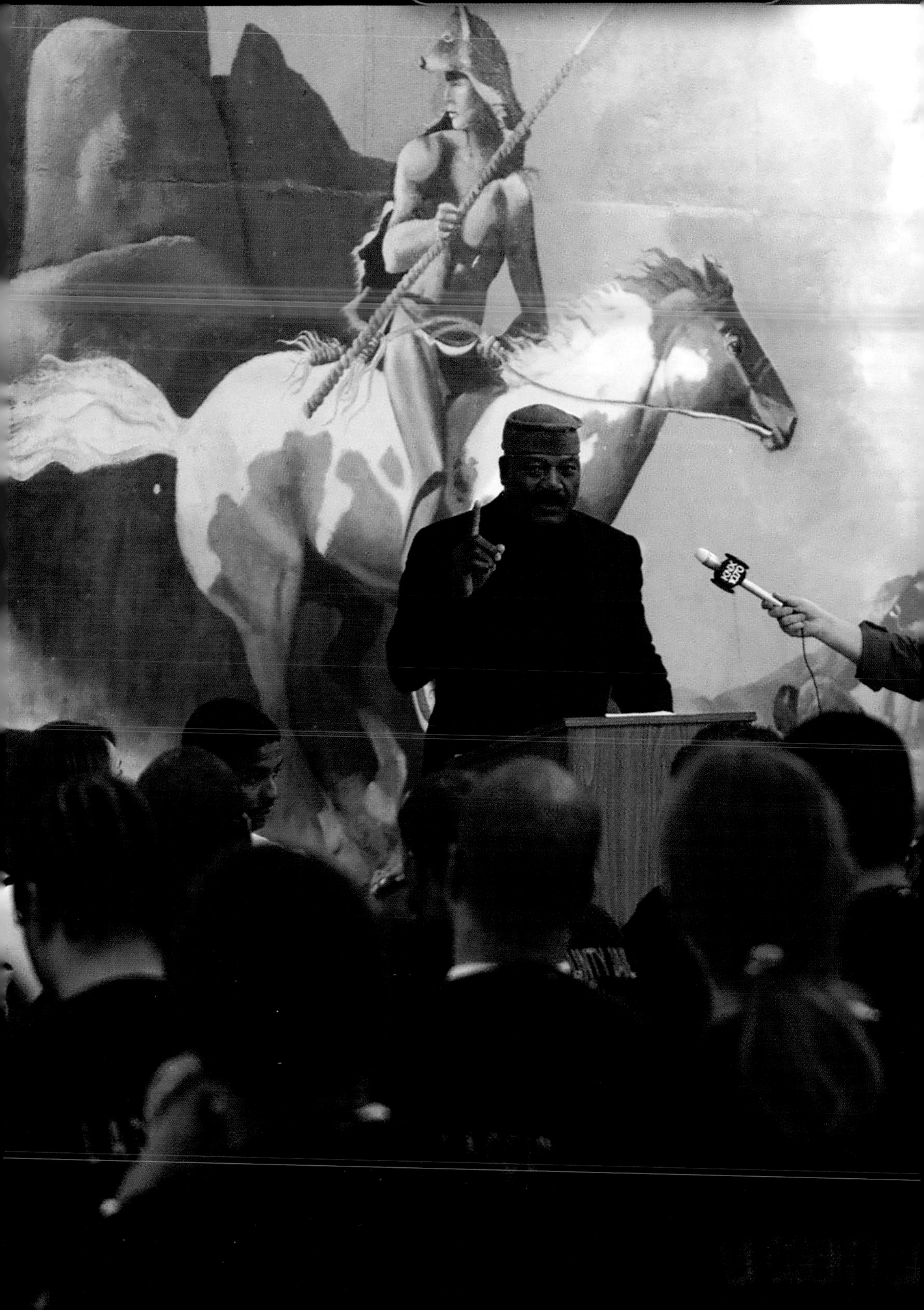

SHOOTING HOOPS, NOT GUNS

During the 2016 presidential campaign, the 1994 Violent Crime Act became a source of debate. Democratic candidate Hillary Clinton, whose husband Bill had been in the White House at the time of the bill's passing, said she regretted that it passed because it resulted in too many inner city youths winding up in jail.

One unique program, however, did emerge as a positive force. That was midnight basketball, which many cities adopted to take gang members off the streets doing something they enjoyed. It received great criticism from conservatives and strong support from liberals. "Midnight basketball was described as paying money so that (drug addicts) could play basketball in the middle of the night," said Virginia Democratic congressman Bobby Scott. "What they left out was the fact that every time they put midnight basketball in a neighborhood, the crime rate plummeted."

By mid-August of 1994, midnight basketball was operating in forty-five cities. However, funding for the program never fully materialized because of the political bickering, according to Carrie Johnson's 2014 report for NPR.

In the summer of 2015, at least one city revived it, and that was Providence, Rhode Island. According to Bill Reynolds for *Providence Journal*, it gained such popularity that there all thirty-two teams were filled and some interested kids had to be turned away. Every player received a free pair of sneakers. Vendors sold food near the outdoor courts. A state police officer was assigned to every game to stop any violence that may have occured before it started.

Midnight basketball programs such as this one played a role in keeping kids out of gangs and off the streets.

The mission statement of Amer-I-Can is the belief that a poor self-image and negative personal development produce criminal behavior. Its intent is to introduce kids to self-determination and motivate them through reachable goals. Young people can then achieve emotional and financial success without gangs. It teaches them in an honest and straightforward way why their past behavioral issues have negatively affected their lives. Eventually self-doubt transforms into self-reliance.

Perhaps you don't fit the description of those whose past behavioral problems have placed themselves on a path to destruction. But you can utilize other resources that allow you to look inward and better understand yourself. Mental health professionals can help with a myriad of psychological and emotional issues you might be battling. Research has noted many risk factors for gang involvement. Negative family experiences such as physical abuse often result in aggressive tendencies in early childhood like bullying and can lead later to violent eruptions, social problems in school, and volatile relationships. Many teens are unaware of how their upbringing and personality have affected them and brought about issues of self-image and anger that lead them to consider joining a gang.

You should also be aware that exposure at an early age to violence in the neighborhood places youths at a greater risk of gang membership. They feel more threatened because they might see shootings in the street as a result of gang activity and consider themselves to be in danger. But you should also be aware that even those in high-risk areas can be protected by prevention strategies such as improved family function, healthy relationships with friends, and academic success. The inner struggle between right and wrong has been lost at least temporarily by those who join gangs. The National Institute for Justice suggests that your battle should be discussed with a school counselor. He or she might recommend a behavioral therapist or psychologist that could allow you to recognize how your past has affected your present.

FINDING HELP ONLINE

The Internet is also a rich resource where you can find recommendations from experts on avoiding gangs. Among the websites is that of the Violence Prevention Institute, which lists many strategies, some of which encourage involvement in anti-gang initiatives outside your school.

The institute stresses that you should inform a responsible and trusted adult such as a parent, neighbor, or police officer if you feel threatened. It lists a number of tips, including not wearing gang colors (particularly where gang members hang out), avoiding dangerous where you are aware of criminal activity, and avoiding drugs, alcohol, physical confrontations, and bullying. The institute also urges you to participate in positive activities and not stay out too late. Gangs often partake in many of their criminal activities late at night.

Graffiti is just one of many signs of gang activity in a neighborhood.

The Violence Prevention Institute also recommends action that can weaken gang control in your neighborhood. Such activities can make you feel like you are part of the solution rather than part of the problem. It can be argued that those who do nothing are helping gangs thrive through their inaction.

Its strongest recommendations go beyond finding healthy ways to spend time and energy and staying away from gang members. The institute urges youths not to carry guns or other weapon because they escalate conflicts and increase the chances that they will be harmed or even killed. Those who fear that they're in danger should contact the police and take precautions for their safety, such as avoiding being alone in public, staying home, or hanging out with a group of friends who aren't associated with gangs. Also encouraged is personal involvement, such as finding out about gang recruitment, activity, signs, and colors, then sharing the information by publishing an article in the school or local newspaper while staying anonymous. You might also speak with community groups and concerned parents, but it's important to make certain that gangs don't learn your identity.

The Violence Prevention Institute also suggests joining an existing group that's working to eliminate gangs in your school or community or to even

Community programs that offer sports and other healthy activities to youth are critical to keeping them out of gangs.

starting your own campaign. Among the methods of achieving that is through the launching of a neighborhood watch group or community patrol. You can report suspicious activity to police while starting or joining a program to remove gang graffiti from walls and buildings.

Those open to looking for organizations and resources can examine the National Youth Network website, which is affiliated with the Office of Juvenile Justice and Delinquency Prevention. The site explains how to plan and start an anti-gang program.

Research has proved that the seeds of gang affiliation are often planted in young children through the witnessing or victimization of violence in the home and neighborhood. You can help prevent kids, particularly younger siblings, from joining a gang by being proactive. Many troubled youngsters feeling unloved eventually join gangs because they perceive them to be the caring family that has been missing throughout their lives. You need not raise the issue of gang life to a young child to show him or her that you care. Spending time partaking in a positive, enjoyable activity with the child can achieve that goal. If the youngster is old enough to know about gangs and shows a curiosity, you can be the one that lays down a path of success in the opposite direction.

GETTING INVOLVED—OR NOT

Knowledge is one of many keys to independence and self-determination. Your involvement in anti-gang programs in your community allows you to learn more about the dangers of gangs, thereby separating you further from any thoughts of joining. But you might feel most comfortable with just saying no to gangs and forging a positive and healthy lifestyle. The most important goal is to remain gang-free. You must decide what is best for you.

Staying away from guns is one of the best things you can decide to do. If a friend carries a gun, it puts you in danger. Gang members often carry guns and use them when arguments escalate, especially if drugs or alcohol are involved. Research shows that about 80 percent of people killed with a gun knew the person who pulled the trigger. Let your friends know your conviction that carrying a gun is not cool, then separate yourself from them until they get rid of it.

You might be thinking of getting a gun for protection if you fear gangs or have made the mistake of joining. But you can protect yourself in other ways. When someone carries a gun, it's more likely to be used against him or someone he knows rather than the unknown attacker. So walk in well-lit areas and with other people. Take a self-defense class to gain the skill and confidence to fight off an attack.

A far safer approach is to use violence only as a last resort to resolve a conflict. Learn about conflict mediation and resolution, then teach your friends. The Violence Prevention Institute has resources for this too. It takes more courage to avoid a fight than it does to escalate one.

None of this should be necessary if you simply say no to gangs. But if you have taken that fateful step, a number of options are available to you. Among them is to inform your fellow gang members politely and firmly of your desire to get out. Speak with a trusted family member about your resolution. Discuss your situation with a school counselor.

Threats are rarely made and infrequently carried out. Again, Michelle Arciaga Young's study has shown that most are able to leave gangs without the threat of violence. Interviews with former gang members revealed that 91 percent simply left without incident. But if you are threatened with "departure rituals" that could cause serious injury or even death, contact a police officer as soon as possible.

Other steps should be taken if you seek to make a clean break. One is to simply spend your time pursuing other interests, such as sports and recreation, music, art, drama, or whatever intrigues you. Another is to spend more time with uplifting and supportive family members and friends.

Stop buying into the edgy image of a gang member. Shed yourself of gang clothing and colors. No more flashing of gang signs and using gang symbols. Be an individual. You don't need to be affiliated with a group who brings you nothing but misery and danger to bolster your self-esteem. Stop hanging out with gang members. Perhaps you will still receive calls or visits from them. Let them know you are no longer interested.

If they want to spend time with you, tell them you are doing something else. It will be the truth.

You are special. You deserve a life that is healthy and gratifying. Only you can make it happen. Joining a gang puts you on a path to nowhere but self-destruction and possibly death. But walking on a path of freedom and positivity brings pride and hope for the future.

GLOSSARY

adolescent A young person during the period between puberty and adulthood.

alienation Being indifferent or causing harm to another person.

antisocial Being unable or unwilling to communicate with other people.

conformity An attempt to act, dress, and think like others in a group.

delinquency Illegal acts and behavior usually associated with young people.

diversion A distraction from business through recreation or other activities.

dysfunctional Not working properly or effectively, often cited as a family issue.

homicide The act of murdering another person.

initiative Taking the first step in reaching a goal.

intervention Becoming involved in an issue to help achieve positive change.

manipulation To skillfully and often unfairly work to manage people or situations to get what one wants.

precocious Behavioral development that is advanced or mature negatively or positively.

predisposed To have an inclination or tendency beforehand.

rationalize To create an untrue belief or excuse that is expressed or in one's own mind.

socioeconomic A combination of social and economic factors often used to explain issues.

superficial A person that is shallow or fake.

supervision The act of overseeing a job or the actions of another person.

tendency A natural or prevailing disposition to act or react a certain way.

victimization To be fooled, cheated, or physically beaten.

vulnerability Greatly susceptible to being emotionally or physically hurt.

FOR MORE INFORMATION

Amer-I-Can Program
269 South Beverly Drive, #1048
Los Angeles, CA 90212
Website: http://www.amer-i-can.org/contact/contact.html

This program works to empower youths and keep them out of gangs while giving them the life skills needed to succeed

Boys & Girls Clubs of America
1821 Middle Avenue
Elyria, OH 44035
(440) 328-3226

The Boys & Girls Clubs provide opportunities for kids to stay off the streets while engaging in many worthwhile activities and programs that prove the community cares about them.

Kids Help Phone Canada
300-439 University Avenue
Toronto, ON M5G 1Y8
Canada
416-586-5437
Ontario@kidshelpphone.ca

This agency provides help around the clock for young people experiencing a wide range of issues.

National Association of Police Athletics/Activities
Leagues
1662 North Highway 1, Suite C
Jupiter, FL 33469
(561) 745-5535

This organization gives youths an opportunity to participate in many athletic and other activities. The purpose is to improve self-image and self-reliance while keeping kids out of gangs.

National Crime Prevention Council (NCPC)
2614 Chapel Lake Drive, Suite B
Gambrills, MD 21054
(443) 292-4565

The NCPC seeks to help people keep themselves, their families, and their communities safe from crime. To achieve that goal, it produces tools that communities can use to learn crime prevention strategies.

National Gang Center
PO Box 12729
Tallahassee, FL 32317
(850) 385-0600
Website: https://www.nationalgangcenter.gov

This organization works to further the mission of the United States Department of Justice by providing wide-ranging information and resources on gangs.

Office of Juvenile Justice and Delinquent Prevention
   (OJJDP)
PO Box 6000
Rockville, MD 20849-6000
(800) 851-3420

The OJJDP works seeks to fight against gangs through research, programs, and training initiatives while setting policies to guide federal juvenile justice issues.

Youth Against Violence Line

1-800-680-4264

Websites: http://youthagainstviolenceline.com

This Canadian service allows anyone concerned about their safety or the safety of others to call and speak confidentially. Callers receive information and assistance.

WEBSITES

Because of the changing nature of internet links, Rosen Publishing has developed an online list of websites related to the subject of this book. This site is updated regularly. Please use this link to access this list:

http://www.rosenlinks.com/411/gang

FOR FURTHER READING

Balk, David E. *Dealing with Dying, Death, and Grief During Adolescence*. New York, NY: Routledge, 2014

Berlatsky, Noah (Ed.). *Gangs*. Farmington Hills, MI: Greenhaven Press, 2015

Brotherton, David. *Youth Street Gangs: A Critical Appraisal*. New York, NY: Routledge, 2015

Covey, Herbert C. *Crips and Bloods: A Guide to an American Subculture*. Santa Barbara, CA: Greenwood Press, 2015

Curry, David G. *Confronting Gangs: Crime and Community*. New York, NY: Oxford University Press, 2014

Delaney, Tim. *American Street Gangs*. Boston, MA: Pearson, 2014

Ewing, Lynne. *The Lure*. New York, NY: Balzer & Bray, 2014

Franzese, Robert J. *Youth Gangs*. Springfield, IL: Charles C. Thomas, 2016

Head, Honor. *How to Handle Bullying and Gangs*. Mankato, MN: Smart Apple Media, 2015

Howell, James C. *Gangs in America's Communities*. Los Angeles, CA: Sage Publications, 2016

Howell, James C. *The History of Street Gangs in the United States: Their Origins and Transformations*. Lanham, MA: Lexington Books, 2015

Jones, Patrick. *Target*. Minneapolis, MN: Darby Creek, 2014

Klein, Malcolm W. *Chasing After Street Gangs: A Forty Year Journey*. New York, NY: Oxford University Press, 2016

Mullen, Diane C. *Tagged*. Watertown, MA: Charlesbridge, 2015

Pevec, Illene. *Growing a Life: Teen Gardeners Harvest Food, Health, and Joy*. New York, NY: New Village Press, 2016

Sanders, Bill. *Gangs: An Introduction*. New York, NY: Oxford University Press, 2016

Sommer, Carl. *Dare to Dream!* Houston, TX: Advance Publishing, Inc., 2014

Tullson, Diane. *Foolproof*. Custer, WA: Orca Book Publishers, 2015

Voloj, Julian. *Ghetto Brother: Warrior to Peacemaker*. New York, NY: NBM Comics Lit, 2015

Wolny, Phillip. *Defeating Gangs in Your Neighborhood and Online*. New York, NY: Rosen Publishing, 2016

BIBLIOGRAPHY

American Academy of Child & Adolescent Psychiatry. "Gangs and Children," August 2011. https://www.aacap.org/AACAP/Families_and_Youth/Facts_for_Families/FFF-Guide/Children-and-Gangs-098.aspx.

The Amer-I-Can Program. http://www.amer-i-can.org/about/about.html.

BBC News. "Truce that Ended 30 years of LA Gang Warfare." April 15, 2015. http://www.bbc.com/news/magazine-32250743.

Carlie, Mike. Excerpts from *Into the Abyss: A Personal Journey into the World of Street Gangs*. Part 15: Getting Out of a Gang. 2002. http://people.missouristate.edu/michaelcarlie/what_i_learned_about/gangs/getting_out_of_a_gang.htm.

Esbensen, Finn-Aage. "Evaluating G.R.E.A.T.: A School-Based Gang Prevention Program." National Institute of Justice, June 2004. https://www.ncjrs.gov/pdffiles1/198604.pdf.

Gang Resistance Education and Training. "What is G.R.E.A.T.?" https://www.great-online.org/Home/About/What-Is-GREAT.

Healthy ATC. "Boys and Girls Club Gang Prevention Through Targeted Outreach." http://www.healthyatc.org/index.php?controller=index&module=PromisePractice&action=view&pid=874.

Howell, James C. "Gang Prevention: An Overview of

Research and Programs." Office of Juvenile Justice and Delinquency Prevention: Juvenile Justice Bulletin, December 2010. https://www.ncjrs.gov/pdffiles1/ojjdp/231116.pdf.

Iowa State University. "Violent video games are a risk factor for criminal behavior and aggression." March 26, 2013. Accessed August 2, 2016. http://www.news.iastate.edu/news/2013/03/26/violentvideogames.

Issurdatt, Sharon. "Gangs: A Growing Problem in Schools." The National Association of Social Workers, September 2011. http://www.naswdc.org/assets/secured/documents/practice/ssw/Gangs%20in%20Schools.pdf.

Johnson, Carrie. "20 Years Later, Parts of Major Crime Bill Viewed as Terrible Mistake." NPR, September 12, 2014. http://www.npr.org/2014/09/12/347736999/20-years-later-major-crime-bill-viewed-as-terrible-mistake.

Journalist's Resource. "U.S. Justice Department: Does Neighborhood Watch Reduce Crime?" March 26, 2012. http://journalistsresource.org/studies/government/criminal-justice/us-justice-department-neighborhood-watch-reduce-crime.

Journal of School Violence. "Evaluation and Evolution of the Gang Resistance and Education Training Program." National Gang Center, 2011. https://www.nationalgangcenter.gov/content/documents/great-evaluation-and-evolution.pdf.

National Association of Police. "Athletic/Activities

League, Inc." http://www.nationalpal.org/Default.aspx?tabid=786286.

National Counter Street Gangs Intelligence. "Gang Myths and Facts." http://www.nationalcsi.org/gang_myths_&_facts.htm.

National Crime Prevention Council. "Keeping Kids Cool & Confident," 2012. http://www.ncpc.org/programs/crime-prevention-month/crime-prevention-month-kits/NCPC-Crime%20Prevention%20Month%20Kit%202012.pdf.

National Gang Center. "National Youth Gang Survey Analysis." https://www.nationalgangcenter.gov/survey-analysis/measuring-the-extent-of-gang-problems.

National Gang Center. "OJJDP Strategic Planning Tool." https://www.nationalgangcenter.gov/SPT/Risk-Factors/FAQ.

National Institute of Justice. "Changing Course: Keeping Kids out of Gangs." http://nij.gov/journals/273/pages/preventing-gang-membership.aspx.

National Neighborhood Watch. "About National Neighborhood Watch. http://www.nnw.org/about-national-neigborhood-watch.

Rew, L., M. Taylor Sheehafter, and M. L. Fitzgerald. "Sexual Abuse, Alcohol and Other Drug Use, and Suicidal Behavior in Homeless Adolescents." US National Library of Medicine/National Institutes of Health, October–December 2001. http://www.ncbi.nlm.nih.gov/pubmed/11769208.

Reynolds, Bill. "Bill Reynolds: Midnight Basketball is

more than just a Providence summer league." *Providence Journal*, August 1, 2015. http://www .providencejournal.com/article/20150801/SPORTS/ 150809850.

Swahn, Monica H., Robert M. Bossarte, Bethany A. West, and Volkan Topalli. "Alcohol and Drug Use Among Gang Members: Experiences of Adolescents Who Attend School." Institute of Public Health, April 15, 2014. https://www.researchgate.net/publication/ 44887862_Alcohol_and_Drug_Use_Among_Gang_ Members_Experiences_of_Adolescents_Who_ Attend_School.

Strategic Planning Tool. "Boys & Girls Club—Gang Prevention Through Targeted Outreach." https:// www.nationalgangcenter.gov/SPT/Programs/67.

Turner, Dawn M. "Ex-gang member talks about rap music's influence." *Chicago Tribune*. November 5, 2015. Accessed August 1, 2016. http://www.chicagotribune .com/news/columnists/ct-rap-music-gang-influence -turner-20151105-column.html

Violence Prevention Institute. "Avoiding Guns, Gangs and Violence." http://www.violencepreventioninstitute .com/avoiding.html.

Young, Michelle Arciaga. "Getting Out of Gangs, Staying Out of Gangs: Gang Intervention and Desistence Strategies." Office of Juvenile Justice and Delinquency Prevention. National Gang Center Bulletin, January 2013. https://www.nationalgangcenter.gov/Content/ Documents/Getting-Out-Staying-Out.pdf.

INDEX

ABOUT THE AUTHOR

Martin Gitlin is an educational book author based in Cleveland, Ohio. He has had more than one hundred educational books published since 2006. As a newspaper journalist from 1991 to 2002 he won more than forty-five awards, including first place for general excellence from the Associated Press, which selected him as one of the top four feature writers in Ohio in 2002.

PHOTO CREDITS

Cover, p. 1 Pressmaster/Shutterstock.com; p. 5 Digital Vision/Photodisc/Thinkstock; pp. 6–7, 36–37 John Carey/Photolibrary/Getty Images; pp. 10–11 DreamPictures/Blend Images/Getty Images; pp. 14–15 Mika/Corbis/Getty Images; pp. 22–23 Highwaystarz-Photography/iStock/Thinkstock; p. 27 Image Source/Getty Images; pp. 30–31 DenisTangneyJr/E+/Getty Images; pp. 32–33 Doug Menuez/Photodisc/Thinkstock; p. 39 flil/Shutterstock.com; pp. 46–47 Steve West/Taxi Japan/Getty Images; pp. 48–49 Chuck Savage/Corbis/Getty Images; pp. 50–51 Lathan Goumas/The Herald News/AP Images; pp. 52–53 Bettmann/Getty Images; p. 56 fcscafeine/iStock/Thinkstock; pp. 60–61 Igor_photo/Shutterstock.com; p. 63 © Eric Engman/News-Miner/Fairbanks Daily News-Miner/ZUMAPress.com; pp. 66–67 © AP Images; pp. 70–71 Sara Press/Photolibrary/Getty Images; pp. 74–75 Hero Images/Getty Images; pp. 76–77 The Washington Post/Getty Images; pp. 80–81 Hill Street Studios/Blend Images/Getty Images; p. 85 Myung J. Chun/Los Angeles Times/Getty Images; pp. 86–87 © Globe Photos/ZUMAPress.com; pp. 90–91 A_Lesik/Shutterstock.com; pp. 92–93 Chris Schmidt/E+/Getty Images.

Designer: Les Kanturek; Editor: Rachel Gluckstern;
Photo Researcher: Karen Huang